Phone Call Log

This log belongs to

Contact Info

Log #:   Log Start Date:

                          Log End Date:

"I'm a greater believer in luck, and I find the harder I work the more I have of it."

~ Thomas Jefferson

Date:	Time:	AM / PM	From:

Message:

Follow up: | | | **Completed:** ☐

Phone / Fax / Cell: Email:

Company/Address: Urgency: Low / Medium / High

Date:	Time:	AM / PM	From:

Message:

Follow up: | | | **Completed:** ☐

Phone / Fax / Cell: Email:

Company/Address: Urgency: Low / Medium / High

Date:	Time:	AM / PM	From:

Message:

Follow up: | | | **Completed:** ☐

Phone / Fax / Cell: Email:

Company/Address: Urgency: Low / Medium / High

Date:	Time:	AM / PM	From:

Message:

Follow up: | | | **Completed:** ☐

Phone / Fax / Cell: Email:

Company/Address: Urgency: Low / Medium / High

Date:	Time:	AM / PM	From:

Message:

Follow up: | | | **Completed:** ☐

Phone / Fax / Cell: Email:

Company/Address: Urgency: Low / Medium / High

Date: Time: AM / PM   From:

Message:

....

Follow up: **Completed:** ☐

Phone / Fax / Cell: Email:

Company/Address: Urgency: Low / Medium / High

Date: Time: AM / PM   From:

Message:

....

Follow up: **Completed:** ☐

Phone / Fax / Cell: Email:

Company/Address: Urgency: Low / Medium / High

Date: Time: AM / PM   From:

Message:

....

Follow up: **Completed:** ☐

Phone / Fax / Cell: Email:

Company/Address: Urgency: Low / Medium / High

Date: Time: AM / PM   From:

Message:

....

Follow up: **Completed:** ☐

Phone / Fax / Cell: Email:

Company/Address: Urgency: Low / Medium / High

Date: Time: AM / PM   From:

Message:

....

Follow up: **Completed:** ☐

Phone / Fax / Cell: Email:

Company/Address: Urgency: Low / Medium / High

Date: Time: AM / PM   From:

Message:

Follow up:				Completed:	☐
Phone / Fax / Cell:		Email:			
Company/Address:			Urgency:	Low / Medium / High	

Date: Time: AM / PM   From:

Message:

Follow up:				Completed:	☐
Phone / Fax / Cell:		Email:			
Company/Address:			Urgency:	Low / Medium / High	

Date: Time: AM / PM   From:

Message:

Follow up:				Completed:	☐
Phone / Fax / Cell:		Email:			
Company/Address:			Urgency:	Low / Medium / High	

Date: Time: AM / PM   From:

Message:

Follow up:				Completed:	☐
Phone / Fax / Cell:		Email:			
Company/Address:			Urgency:	Low / Medium / High	

Date: Time: AM / PM   From:

Message:

Follow up:				Completed:	☐
Phone / Fax / Cell:		Email:			
Company/Address:			Urgency:	Low / Medium / High	

Date: Time: AM / PM   From:
Message:

Follow up: **Completed:**
Phone / Fax / Cell: Email:
Company/Address: Urgency: Low / Medium / High

Date: Time: AM / PM   From:
Message:

Follow up: **Completed:**
Phone / Fax / Cell: Email:
Company/Address: Urgency: Low / Medium / High

Date: Time: AM / PM   From:
Message:

Follow up: **Completed:**
Phone / Fax / Cell: Email:
Company/Address: Urgency: Low / Medium / High

Date: Time: AM / PM   From:
Message:

Follow up: **Completed:**
Phone / Fax / Cell: Email:
Company/Address: Urgency: Low / Medium / High

Date: Time: AM / PM   From:
Message:

Follow up: **Completed:**
Phone / Fax / Cell: Email:
Company/Address: Urgency: Low / Medium / High

Date:	Time:	AM / PM	From:

Message:

Follow up:			Completed: ☐
Phone / Fax / Cell:		Email:	
Company/Address:		Urgency:	Low / Medium / High

Date:	Time:	AM / PM	From:

Message:

Follow up:			Completed: ☐
Phone / Fax / Cell:		Email:	
Company/Address:		Urgency:	Low / Medium / High

Date:	Time:	AM / PM	From:

Message:

Follow up:			Completed: ☐
Phone / Fax / Cell:		Email:	
Company/Address:		Urgency:	Low / Medium / High

Date:	Time:	AM / PM	From:

Message:

Follow up:			Completed: ☐
Phone / Fax / Cell:		Email:	
Company/Address:		Urgency:	Low / Medium / High

Date:	Time:	AM / PM	From:

Message:

Follow up:			Completed: ☐
Phone / Fax / Cell:		Email:	
Company/Address:		Urgency:	Low / Medium / High

Date:	Time:	AM / PM	From:

Message:

Follow up: Completed: ☐

Phone / Fax / Cell: Email:

Company/Address: Urgency: Low / Medium / High

Date:	Time:	AM / PM	From:

Message:

Follow up: Completed: ☐

Phone / Fax / Cell: Email:

Company/Address: Urgency: Low / Medium / High

Date:	Time:	AM / PM	From:

Message:

Follow up: Completed: ☐

Phone / Fax / Cell: Email:

Company/Address: Urgency: Low / Medium / High

Date:	Time:	AM / PM	From:

Message:

Follow up: Completed: ☐

Phone / Fax / Cell: Email:

Company/Address: Urgency: Low / Medium / High

Date:	Time:	AM / PM	From:

Message:

Follow up: Completed: ☐

Phone / Fax / Cell: Email:

Company/Address: Urgency: Low / Medium / High

Date: Time: AM / PM   From:

Message:

Follow up:			Completed: ☐
Phone / Fax / Cell:		Email:	
Company/Address:		Urgency:	Low / Medium / High

Date: Time: AM / PM   From:

Message:

Follow up:			Completed: ☐
Phone / Fax / Cell:		Email:	
Company/Address:		Urgency:	Low / Medium / High

Date: Time: AM / PM   From:

Message:

Follow up:			Completed: ☐
Phone / Fax / Cell:		Email:	
Company/Address:		Urgency:	Low / Medium / High

Date: Time: AM / PM   From:

Message:

Follow up:			Completed: ☐
Phone / Fax / Cell:		Email:	
Company/Address:		Urgency:	Low / Medium / High

Date: Time: AM / PM   From:

Message:

Follow up:			Completed: ☐
Phone / Fax / Cell:		Email:	
Company/Address:		Urgency:	Low / Medium / High

Date:					Time:				AM / PM		From:
Message:

Follow up:							**Completed:**
Phone / Fax / Cell:				Email:
Company/Address:						Urgency:	Low / Medium / High

Date:					Time:				AM / PM		From:
Message:

Follow up:							**Completed:**
Phone / Fax / Cell:				Email:
Company/Address:						Urgency:	Low / Medium / High

Date:					Time:				AM / PM		From:
Message:

Follow up:							**Completed:**
Phone / Fax / Cell:				Email:
Company/Address:						Urgency:	Low / Medium / High

Date:					Time:				AM / PM		From:
Message:

Follow up:							**Completed:**
Phone / Fax / Cell:				Email:
Company/Address:						Urgency:	Low / Medium / High

Date:					Time:				AM / PM		From:
Message:

Follow up:							**Completed:**
Phone / Fax / Cell:				Email:
Company/Address:						Urgency:	Low / Medium / High

Date:					Time:					AM / PM		From:

Message:

Follow up:					Completed:	☐

Phone / Fax / Cell:					Email:

Company/Address:					Urgency:		Low / Medium / High

Date:					Time:					AM / PM		From:

Message:

Follow up:					Completed:	☐

Phone / Fax / Cell:					Email:

Company/Address:					Urgency:		Low / Medium / High

Date:					Time:					AM / PM		From:

Message:

Follow up:					Completed:	☐

Phone / Fax / Cell:					Email:

Company/Address:					Urgency:		Low / Medium / High

Date:					Time:					AM / PM		From:

Message:

Follow up:					Completed:	☐

Phone / Fax / Cell:					Email:

Company/Address:					Urgency:		Low / Medium / High

Date:					Time:					AM / PM		From:

Message:

Follow up:					Completed:	☐

Phone / Fax / Cell:					Email:

Company/Address:					Urgency:		Low / Medium / High

Date: Time: AM / PM   From:
Message:

Follow up: **Completed:** ☐
Phone / Fax / Cell: Email:
Company/Address: Urgency: Low / Medium / High

Date: Time: AM / PM   From:
Message:

Follow up: **Completed:** ☐
Phone / Fax / Cell: Email:
Company/Address: Urgency: Low / Medium / High

Date: Time: AM / PM   From:
Message:

Follow up: **Completed:** ☐
Phone / Fax / Cell: Email:
Company/Address: Urgency: Low / Medium / High

Date: Time: AM / PM   From:
Message:

Follow up: **Completed:** ☐
Phone / Fax / Cell: Email:
Company/Address: Urgency: Low / Medium / High

Date: Time: AM / PM   From:
Message:

Follow up: **Completed:** ☐
Phone / Fax / Cell: Email:
Company/Address: Urgency: Low / Medium / High

Date: Time: AM / PM   From:

Message:

Follow up:			Completed: ☐
Phone / Fax / Cell:		Email:	
Company/Address:		Urgency:	Low / Medium / High

Date: Time: AM / PM   From:

Message:

Follow up:			Completed: ☐
Phone / Fax / Cell:		Email:	
Company/Address:		Urgency:	Low / Medium / High

Date: Time: AM / PM   From:

Message:

Follow up:			Completed: ☐
Phone / Fax / Cell:		Email:	
Company/Address:		Urgency:	Low / Medium / High

Date: Time: AM / PM   From:

Message:

Follow up:			Completed: ☐
Phone / Fax / Cell:		Email:	
Company/Address:		Urgency:	Low / Medium / High

Date: Time: AM / PM   From:

Message:

Follow up:			Completed: ☐
Phone / Fax / Cell:		Email:	
Company/Address:		Urgency:	Low / Medium / High

Date: Time: AM / PM   From:
Message:

Follow up:				Completed:	☐

Phone / Fax / Cell: Email:
Company/Address: Urgency: Low / Medium / High

Date: Time: AM / PM   From:
Message:

Follow up:				Completed:	☐

Phone / Fax / Cell: Email:
Company/Address: Urgency: Low / Medium / High

Date: Time: AM / PM   From:
Message:

Follow up:				Completed:	☐

Phone / Fax / Cell: Email:
Company/Address: Urgency: Low / Medium / High

Date: Time: AM / PM   From:
Message:

Follow up:				Completed:	☐

Phone / Fax / Cell: Email:
Company/Address: Urgency: Low / Medium / High

Date: Time: AM / PM   From:
Message:

Follow up:				Completed:	☐

Phone / Fax / Cell: Email:
Company/Address: Urgency: Low / Medium / High

Date:	Time:	AM / PM	From:

Message:

Follow up:					Completed:	☐
Phone / Fax / Cell:			Email:			
Company/Address:				Urgency:	Low / Medium / High	

Date:	Time:	AM / PM	From:

Message:

Follow up:					Completed:	☐
Phone / Fax / Cell:			Email:			
Company/Address:				Urgency:	Low / Medium / High	

Date:	Time:	AM / PM	From:

Message:

Follow up:					Completed:	☐
Phone / Fax / Cell:			Email:			
Company/Address:				Urgency:	Low / Medium / High	

Date:	Time:	AM / PM	From:

Message:

Follow up:					Completed:	☐
Phone / Fax / Cell:			Email:			
Company/Address:				Urgency:	Low / Medium / High	

Date:	Time:	AM / PM	From:

Message:

Follow up:					Completed:	☐
Phone / Fax / Cell:			Email:			
Company/Address:				Urgency:	Low / Medium / High	

Date:　　　　　　　Time:　　　　　　　AM / PM　From:
Message:

Follow up:　　　　　　　　　　　　　　　　　　　　　**Completed:** ☐
Phone / Fax / Cell:　　　　　　　　　　Email:
Company/Address:　　　　　　　　　　　　　　Urgency:　Low / Medium / High

Date:　　　　　　　Time:　　　　　　　AM / PM　From:
Message:

Follow up:　　　　　　　　　　　　　　　　　　　　　**Completed:** ☐
Phone / Fax / Cell:　　　　　　　　　　Email:
Company/Address:　　　　　　　　　　　　　　Urgency:　Low / Medium / High

Date:　　　　　　　Time:　　　　　　　AM / PM　From:
Message:

Follow up:　　　　　　　　　　　　　　　　　　　　　**Completed:** ☐
Phone / Fax / Cell:　　　　　　　　　　Email:
Company/Address:　　　　　　　　　　　　　　Urgency:　Low / Medium / High

Date:　　　　　　　Time:　　　　　　　AM / PM　From:
Message:

Follow up:　　　　　　　　　　　　　　　　　　　　　**Completed:** ☐
Phone / Fax / Cell:　　　　　　　　　　Email:
Company/Address:　　　　　　　　　　　　　　Urgency:　Low / Medium / High

Date:　　　　　　　Time:　　　　　　　AM / PM　From:
Message:

Follow up:　　　　　　　　　　　　　　　　　　　　　**Completed:** ☐
Phone / Fax / Cell:　　　　　　　　　　Email:
Company/Address:　　　　　　　　　　　　　　Urgency:　Low / Medium / High

Date:	Time:	AM / PM	From:
Message:

Follow up:			Completed:	☐
Phone / Fax / Cell:		Email:		
Company/Address:			Urgency: Low / Medium / High	

Date:	Time:	AM / PM	From:
Message:

Follow up:			Completed:	☐
Phone / Fax / Cell:		Email:		
Company/Address:			Urgency: Low / Medium / High	

Date:	Time:	AM / PM	From:
Message:

Follow up:			Completed:	☐
Phone / Fax / Cell:		Email:		
Company/Address:			Urgency: Low / Medium / High	

Date:	Time:	AM / PM	From:
Message:

Follow up:			Completed:	☐
Phone / Fax / Cell:		Email:		
Company/Address:			Urgency: Low / Medium / High	

Date:	Time:	AM / PM	From:
Message:

Follow up:			Completed:	☐
Phone / Fax / Cell:		Email:		
Company/Address:			Urgency: Low / Medium / High	

Date: Time: AM / PM   From:
Message:

Follow up: **Completed:** ☐
Phone / Fax / Cell: Email:
Company/Address: Urgency: Low / Medium / High

Date: Time: AM / PM   From:
Message:

Follow up: **Completed:** ☐
Phone / Fax / Cell: Email:
Company/Address: Urgency: Low / Medium / High

Date: Time: AM / PM   From:
Message:

Follow up: **Completed:** ☐
Phone / Fax / Cell: Email:
Company/Address: Urgency: Low / Medium / High

Date: Time: AM / PM   From:
Message:

Follow up: **Completed:** ☐
Phone / Fax / Cell: Email:
Company/Address: Urgency: Low / Medium / High

Date: Time: AM / PM   From:
Message:

Follow up: **Completed:** ☐
Phone / Fax / Cell: Email:
Company/Address: Urgency: Low / Medium / High

| Date: | Time: | AM / PM | From: |

Message:

Follow up: Completed: ☐

Phone / Fax / Cell: Email:

Company/Address: Urgency: Low / Medium / High

| Date: | Time: | AM / PM | From: |

Message:

Follow up: Completed: ☐

Phone / Fax / Cell: Email:

Company/Address: Urgency: Low / Medium / High

| Date: | Time: | AM / PM | From: |

Message:

Follow up: Completed: ☐

Phone / Fax / Cell: Email:

Company/Address: Urgency: Low / Medium / High

| Date: | Time: | AM / PM | From: |

Message:

Follow up: Completed: ☐

Phone / Fax / Cell: Email:

Company/Address: Urgency: Low / Medium / High

| Date: | Time: | AM / PM | From: |

Message:

Follow up: Completed: ☐

Phone / Fax / Cell: Email:

Company/Address: Urgency: Low / Medium / High

Date:	Time:	AM / PM	From:

Message:

Follow up: **Completed:** ☐

Phone / Fax / Cell: Email:

Company/Address: Urgency: Low / Medium / High

Date:	Time:	AM / PM	From:

Message:

Follow up: **Completed:** ☐

Phone / Fax / Cell: Email:

Company/Address: Urgency: Low / Medium / High

Date:	Time:	AM / PM	From:

Message:

Follow up: **Completed:** ☐

Phone / Fax / Cell: Email:

Company/Address: Urgency: Low / Medium / High

Date:	Time:	AM / PM	From:

Message:

Follow up: **Completed:** ☐

Phone / Fax / Cell: Email:

Company/Address: Urgency: Low / Medium / High

Date:	Time:	AM / PM	From:

Message:

Follow up: **Completed:** ☐

Phone / Fax / Cell: Email:

Company/Address: Urgency: Low / Medium / High

Date:					Time:			AM / PM		From:
Message:

| Follow up: | | | | | Completed: | ☐ |

Phone / Fax / Cell:					Email:
Company/Address:						Urgency:	Low / Medium / High

Date:					Time:			AM / PM		From:
Message:

| Follow up: | | | | | Completed: | ☐ |

Phone / Fax / Cell:					Email:
Company/Address:						Urgency:	Low / Medium / High

Date:					Time:			AM / PM		From:
Message:

| Follow up: | | | | | Completed: | ☐ |

Phone / Fax / Cell:					Email:
Company/Address:						Urgency:	Low / Medium / High

Date:					Time:			AM / PM		From:
Message:

| Follow up: | | | | | Completed: | ☐ |

Phone / Fax / Cell:					Email:
Company/Address:						Urgency:	Low / Medium / High

Date:					Time:			AM / PM		From:
Message:

| Follow up: | | | | | Completed: | ☐ |

Phone / Fax / Cell:					Email:
Company/Address:						Urgency:	Low / Medium / High

Date: Time: AM / PM   From:
Message:

Follow up: Completed: ☐
Phone / Fax / Cell: Email:
Company/Address: Urgency: Low / Medium / High

Date: Time: AM / PM   From:
Message:

Follow up: Completed: ☐
Phone / Fax / Cell: Email:
Company/Address: Urgency: Low / Medium / High

Date: Time: AM / PM   From:
Message:

Follow up: Completed: ☐
Phone / Fax / Cell: Email:
Company/Address: Urgency: Low / Medium / High

Date: Time: AM / PM   From:
Message:

Follow up: Completed: ☐
Phone / Fax / Cell: Email:
Company/Address: Urgency: Low / Medium / High

Date: Time: AM / PM   From:
Message:

Follow up: Completed: ☐
Phone / Fax / Cell: Email:
Company/Address: Urgency: Low / Medium / High

| Date: | Time: | AM / PM | From: |

Message:

Follow up: Completed: ☐

Phone / Fax / Cell: Email:

Company/Address: Urgency: Low / Medium / High

| Date: | Time: | AM / PM | From: |

Message:

Follow up: Completed: ☐

Phone / Fax / Cell: Email:

Company/Address: Urgency: Low / Medium / High

| Date: | Time: | AM / PM | From: |

Message:

Follow up: Completed: ☐

Phone / Fax / Cell: Email:

Company/Address: Urgency: Low / Medium / High

| Date: | Time: | AM / PM | From: |

Message:

Follow up: Completed: ☐

Phone / Fax / Cell: Email:

Company/Address: Urgency: Low / Medium / High

| Date: | Time: | AM / PM | From: |

Message:

Follow up: Completed: ☐

Phone / Fax / Cell: Email:

Company/Address: Urgency: Low / Medium / High

Date:					Time:			AM / PM		From:
Message:

Follow up:							Completed: ☐
Phone / Fax / Cell:				Email:
Company/Address:					Urgency:	Low / Medium / High

Date:					Time:			AM / PM		From:
Message:

Follow up:							Completed: ☐
Phone / Fax / Cell:				Email:
Company/Address:					Urgency:	Low / Medium / High

Date:					Time:			AM / PM		From:
Message:

Follow up:							Completed: ☐
Phone / Fax / Cell:				Email:
Company/Address:					Urgency:	Low / Medium / High

Date:					Time:			AM / PM		From:
Message:

Follow up:							Completed: ☐
Phone / Fax / Cell:				Email:
Company/Address:					Urgency:	Low / Medium / High

Date:					Time:			AM / PM		From:
Message:

Follow up:							Completed: ☐
Phone / Fax / Cell:				Email:
Company/Address:					Urgency:	Low / Medium / High

Date: Time: AM / PM   From:
Message:

Follow up:		Completed: ☐
Phone / Fax / Cell: Email:
Company/Address: Urgency: Low / Medium / High

Date: Time: AM / PM   From:
Message:

Follow up:		Completed: ☐
Phone / Fax / Cell: Email:
Company/Address: Urgency: Low / Medium / High

Date: Time: AM / PM   From:
Message:

Follow up:		Completed: ☐
Phone / Fax / Cell: Email:
Company/Address: Urgency: Low / Medium / High

Date: Time: AM / PM   From:
Message:

Follow up:		Completed: ☐
Phone / Fax / Cell: Email:
Company/Address: Urgency: Low / Medium / High

Date: Time: AM / PM   From:
Message:

Follow up:		Completed: ☐
Phone / Fax / Cell: Email:
Company/Address: Urgency: Low / Medium / High

Date: Time: AM / PM   From:

Message:

Follow up: **Completed:** ☐

Phone / Fax / Cell: Email:

Company/Address: Urgency: Low / Medium / High

Date: Time: AM / PM   From:

Message:

Follow up: **Completed:** ☐

Phone / Fax / Cell: Email:

Company/Address: Urgency: Low / Medium / High

Date: Time: AM / PM   From:

Message:

Follow up: **Completed:** ☐

Phone / Fax / Cell: Email:

Company/Address: Urgency: Low / Medium / High

Date: Time: AM / PM   From:

Message:

Follow up: **Completed:** ☐

Phone / Fax / Cell: Email:

Company/Address: Urgency: Low / Medium / High

Date: Time: AM / PM   From:

Message:

Follow up: **Completed:** ☐

Phone / Fax / Cell: Email:

Company/Address: Urgency: Low / Medium / High

Date: Time: AM / PM   From:

Message:

Follow up: Completed: ☐

Phone / Fax / Cell: Email:

Company/Address: Urgency: Low / Medium / High

Date: Time: AM / PM   From:

Message:

Follow up: Completed: ☐

Phone / Fax / Cell: Email:

Company/Address: Urgency: Low / Medium / High

Date: Time: AM / PM   From:

Message:

Follow up: Completed: ☐

Phone / Fax / Cell: Email:

Company/Address: Urgency: Low / Medium / High

Date: Time: AM / PM   From:

Message:

Follow up: Completed: ☐

Phone / Fax / Cell: Email:

Company/Address: Urgency: Low / Medium / High

Date: Time: AM / PM   From:

Message:

Follow up: Completed: ☐

Phone / Fax / Cell: Email:

Company/Address: Urgency: Low / Medium / High

Date:					Time:			AM / PM		From:
Message:

Follow up:												Completed:
Phone / Fax / Cell:					Email:
Company/Address:						Urgency:	Low / Medium / High

Date:					Time:			AM / PM		From:
Message:

Follow up:												Completed:
Phone / Fax / Cell:					Email:
Company/Address:						Urgency:	Low / Medium / High

Date:					Time:			AM / PM		From:
Message:

Follow up:												Completed:
Phone / Fax / Cell:					Email:
Company/Address:						Urgency:	Low / Medium / High

Date:					Time:			AM / PM		From:
Message:

Follow up:												Completed:
Phone / Fax / Cell:					Email:
Company/Address:						Urgency:	Low / Medium / High

Date:					Time:			AM / PM		From:
Message:

Follow up:												Completed:
Phone / Fax / Cell:					Email:
Company/Address:						Urgency:	Low / Medium / High

Date: Time: AM / PM   From:

Message:

Follow up:		Completed: ☐
Phone / Fax / Cell:	Email:	
Company/Address:	Urgency:	Low / Medium / High

Date: Time: AM / PM   From:

Message:

Follow up:		Completed: ☐
Phone / Fax / Cell:	Email:	
Company/Address:	Urgency:	Low / Medium / High

Date: Time: AM / PM   From:

Message:

Follow up:		Completed: ☐
Phone / Fax / Cell:	Email:	
Company/Address:	Urgency:	Low / Medium / High

Date: Time: AM / PM   From:

Message:

Follow up:		Completed: ☐
Phone / Fax / Cell:	Email:	
Company/Address:	Urgency:	Low / Medium / High

Date: Time: AM / PM   From:

Message:

Follow up:		Completed: ☐
Phone / Fax / Cell:	Email:	
Company/Address:	Urgency:	Low / Medium / High

Date:	Time:	AM / PM	From:

Message:

Follow up: Completed: ☐

Phone / Fax / Cell: Email:
Company/Address: Urgency: Low / Medium / High

Date:	Time:	AM / PM	From:

Message:

Follow up: Completed: ☐

Phone / Fax / Cell: Email:
Company/Address: Urgency: Low / Medium / High

Date:	Time:	AM / PM	From:

Message:

Follow up: Completed: ☐

Phone / Fax / Cell: Email:
Company/Address: Urgency: Low / Medium / High

Date:	Time:	AM / PM	From:

Message:

Follow up: Completed: ☐

Phone / Fax / Cell: Email:
Company/Address: Urgency: Low / Medium / High

Date:	Time:	AM / PM	From:

Message:

Follow up: Completed: ☐

Phone / Fax / Cell: Email:
Company/Address: Urgency: Low / Medium / High

Date: Time: AM / PM   From:
Message:

Follow up:				Completed:	☐
Phone / Fax / Cell:		Email:			
Company/Address:			Urgency:	Low / Medium / High	

Date: Time: AM / PM   From:
Message:

Follow up:				Completed:	☐
Phone / Fax / Cell:		Email:			
Company/Address:			Urgency:	Low / Medium / High	

Date: Time: AM / PM   From:
Message:

Follow up:				Completed:	☐
Phone / Fax / Cell:		Email:			
Company/Address:			Urgency:	Low / Medium / High	

Date: Time: AM / PM   From:
Message:

Follow up:				Completed:	☐
Phone / Fax / Cell:		Email:			
Company/Address:			Urgency:	Low / Medium / High	

Date: Time: AM / PM   From:
Message:

Follow up:				Completed:	☐
Phone / Fax / Cell:		Email:			
Company/Address:			Urgency:	Low / Medium / High	

Date:　　　　　　　　Time:　　　　　　　AM / PM　From:

Message:

Follow up:			Completed:	☐
Phone / Fax / Cell:		Email:		
Company/Address:			Urgency: Low / Medium / High	

Date:　　　　　　　　Time:　　　　　　　AM / PM　From:

Message:

Follow up:			Completed:	☐
Phone / Fax / Cell:		Email:		
Company/Address:			Urgency: Low / Medium / High	

Date:　　　　　　　　Time:　　　　　　　AM / PM　From:

Message:

Follow up:			Completed:	☐
Phone / Fax / Cell:		Email:		
Company/Address:			Urgency: Low / Medium / High	

Date:　　　　　　　　Time:　　　　　　　AM / PM　From:

Message:

Follow up:			Completed:	☐
Phone / Fax / Cell:		Email:		
Company/Address:			Urgency: Low / Medium / High	

Date:　　　　　　　　Time:　　　　　　　AM / PM　From:

Message:

Follow up:			Completed:	☐
Phone / Fax / Cell:		Email:		
Company/Address:			Urgency: Low / Medium / High	

| Date: | Time: | AM / PM | From: |

Message:

Follow up: Completed: ☐

Phone / Fax / Cell: Email:

Company/Address: Urgency: Low / Medium / High

| Date: | Time: | AM / PM | From: |

Message:

Follow up: Completed: ☐

Phone / Fax / Cell: Email:

Company/Address: Urgency: Low / Medium / High

| Date: | Time: | AM / PM | From: |

Message:

Follow up: Completed: ☐

Phone / Fax / Cell: Email:

Company/Address: Urgency: Low / Medium / High

| Date: | Time: | AM / PM | From: |

Message:

Follow up: Completed: ☐

Phone / Fax / Cell: Email:

Company/Address: Urgency: Low / Medium / High

| Date: | Time: | AM / PM | From: |

Message:

Follow up: Completed: ☐

Phone / Fax / Cell: Email:

Company/Address: Urgency: Low / Medium / High

Date: Time: AM / PM   From:
Message:

Follow up: Completed: ☐
Phone / Fax / Cell: Email:
Company/Address: Urgency: Low / Medium / High

Date: Time: AM / PM   From:
Message:

Follow up: Completed: ☐
Phone / Fax / Cell: Email:
Company/Address: Urgency: Low / Medium / High

Date: Time: AM / PM   From:
Message:

Follow up: Completed: ☐
Phone / Fax / Cell: Email:
Company/Address: Urgency: Low / Medium / High

Date: Time: AM / PM   From:
Message:

Follow up: Completed: ☐
Phone / Fax / Cell: Email:
Company/Address: Urgency: Low / Medium / High

Date: Time: AM / PM   From:
Message:

Follow up: Completed: ☐
Phone / Fax / Cell: Email:
Company/Address: Urgency: Low / Medium / High

| Date: | Time: | AM / PM | From: |

Message:

Follow up: Completed: ☐

Phone / Fax / Cell: Email:

Company/Address: Urgency: Low / Medium / High

| Date: | Time: | AM / PM | From: |

Message:

Follow up: Completed: ☐

Phone / Fax / Cell: Email:

Company/Address: Urgency: Low / Medium / High

| Date: | Time: | AM / PM | From: |

Message:

Follow up: Completed: ☐

Phone / Fax / Cell: Email:

Company/Address: Urgency: Low / Medium / High

| Date: | Time: | AM / PM | From: |

Message:

Follow up: Completed: ☐

Phone / Fax / Cell: Email:

Company/Address: Urgency: Low / Medium / High

| Date: | Time: | AM / PM | From: |

Message:

Follow up: Completed: ☐

Phone / Fax / Cell: Email:

Company/Address: Urgency: Low / Medium / High

| Date: | Time: | AM / PM | From: |

Message:

Follow up: Completed: ☐

Phone / Fax / Cell: Email:
Company/Address: Urgency: Low / Medium / High

| Date: | Time: | AM / PM | From: |

Message:

Follow up: Completed: ☐

Phone / Fax / Cell: Email:
Company/Address: Urgency: Low / Medium / High

| Date: | Time: | AM / PM | From: |

Message:

Follow up: Completed: ☐

Phone / Fax / Cell: Email:
Company/Address: Urgency: Low / Medium / High

| Date: | Time: | AM / PM | From: |

Message:

Follow up: Completed: ☐

Phone / Fax / Cell: Email:
Company/Address: Urgency: Low / Medium / High

| Date: | Time: | AM / PM | From: |

Message:

Follow up: Completed: ☐

Phone / Fax / Cell: Email:
Company/Address: Urgency: Low / Medium / High

Date: Time: AM / PM From:
Message:

Follow up: Completed: ☐
Phone / Fax / Cell: Email:
Company/Address: Urgency: Low / Medium / High

Date: Time: AM / PM From:
Message:

Follow up: Completed: ☐
Phone / Fax / Cell: Email:
Company/Address: Urgency: Low / Medium / High

Date: Time: AM / PM From:
Message:

Follow up: Completed: ☐
Phone / Fax / Cell: Email:
Company/Address: Urgency: Low / Medium / High

Date: Time: AM / PM From:
Message:

Follow up: Completed: ☐
Phone / Fax / Cell: Email:
Company/Address: Urgency: Low / Medium / High

Date: Time: AM / PM From:
Message:

Follow up: Completed: ☐
Phone / Fax / Cell: Email:
Company/Address: Urgency: Low / Medium / High

Date:　　　　　　　　Time:　　　　　　AM / PM　From:

Message:

Follow up:　　　　　　　　　　　　　　　　　　　　　　　Completed: ☐

Phone / Fax / Cell:　　　　　　　　　　　Email:

Company/Address:　　　　　　　　　　　　　　Urgency:　Low / Medium / High

Date:　　　　　　　　Time:　　　　　　AM / PM　From:

Message:

Follow up:　　　　　　　　　　　　　　　　　　　　　　　Completed: ☐

Phone / Fax / Cell:　　　　　　　　　　　Email:

Company/Address:　　　　　　　　　　　　　　Urgency:　Low / Medium / High

Date:　　　　　　　　Time:　　　　　　AM / PM　From:

Message:

Follow up:　　　　　　　　　　　　　　　　　　　　　　　Completed: ☐

Phone / Fax / Cell:　　　　　　　　　　　Email:

Company/Address:　　　　　　　　　　　　　　Urgency:　Low / Medium / High

Date:　　　　　　　　Time:　　　　　　AM / PM　From:

Message:

Follow up:　　　　　　　　　　　　　　　　　　　　　　　Completed: ☐

Phone / Fax / Cell:　　　　　　　　　　　Email:

Company/Address:　　　　　　　　　　　　　　Urgency:　Low / Medium / High

Date:　　　　　　　　Time:　　　　　　AM / PM　From:

Message:

Follow up:　　　　　　　　　　　　　　　　　　　　　　　Completed: ☐

Phone / Fax / Cell:　　　　　　　　　　　Email:

Company/Address:　　　　　　　　　　　　　　Urgency:　Low / Medium / High

Date: Time: AM / PM From:

Message:

Follow up:			Completed:
Phone / Fax / Cell:		Email:	
Company/Address:			Urgency: Low / Medium / High

Date: Time: AM / PM From:

Message:

Follow up:			Completed:
Phone / Fax / Cell:		Email:	
Company/Address:			Urgency: Low / Medium / High

Date: Time: AM / PM From:

Message:

Follow up:			Completed:
Phone / Fax / Cell:		Email:	
Company/Address:			Urgency: Low / Medium / High

Date: Time: AM / PM From:

Message:

Follow up:			Completed:
Phone / Fax / Cell:		Email:	
Company/Address:			Urgency: Low / Medium / High

Date: Time: AM / PM From:

Message:

Follow up:			Completed:
Phone / Fax / Cell:		Email:	
Company/Address:			Urgency: Low / Medium / High

Date: Time: AM / PM From:
Message:

Follow up: Completed: ☐
Phone / Fax / Cell: Email:
Company/Address: Urgency: Low / Medium / High

Date: Time: AM / PM From:
Message:

Follow up: Completed: ☐
Phone / Fax / Cell: Email:
Company/Address: Urgency: Low / Medium / High

Date: Time: AM / PM From:
Message:

Follow up: Completed: ☐
Phone / Fax / Cell: Email:
Company/Address: Urgency: Low / Medium / High

Date: Time: AM / PM From:
Message:

Follow up: Completed: ☐
Phone / Fax / Cell: Email:
Company/Address: Urgency: Low / Medium / High

Date: Time: AM / PM From:
Message:

Follow up: Completed: ☐
Phone / Fax / Cell: Email:
Company/Address: Urgency: Low / Medium / High

Date: Time: AM / PM   From:
Message:

Follow up: Completed: ☐
Phone / Fax / Cell: Email:
Company/Address: Urgency: Low / Medium / High

Date: Time: AM / PM   From:
Message:

Follow up: Completed: ☐
Phone / Fax / Cell: Email:
Company/Address: Urgency: Low / Medium / High

Date: Time: AM / PM   From:
Message:

Follow up: Completed: ☐
Phone / Fax / Cell: Email:
Company/Address: Urgency: Low / Medium / High

Date: Time: AM / PM   From:
Message:

Follow up: Completed: ☐
Phone / Fax / Cell: Email:
Company/Address: Urgency: Low / Medium / High

Date: Time: AM / PM   From:
Message:

Follow up: Completed: ☐
Phone / Fax / Cell: Email:
Company/Address: Urgency: Low / Medium / High

Date:	Time:	AM / PM	From:

Message:

Follow up: Completed: ☐

Phone / Fax / Cell: Email:

Company/Address: Urgency: Low / Medium / High

Date:	Time:	AM / PM	From:

Message:

Follow up: Completed: ☐

Phone / Fax / Cell: Email:

Company/Address: Urgency: Low / Medium / High

Date:	Time:	AM / PM	From:

Message:

Follow up: Completed: ☐

Phone / Fax / Cell: Email:

Company/Address: Urgency: Low / Medium / High

Date:	Time:	AM / PM	From:

Message:

Follow up: Completed: ☐

Phone / Fax / Cell: Email:

Company/Address: Urgency: Low / Medium / High

Date:	Time:	AM / PM	From:

Message:

Follow up: Completed: ☐

Phone / Fax / Cell: Email:

Company/Address: Urgency: Low / Medium / High

Date: Time: AM / PM   From:

Message:

Follow up:					Completed: ☐
Phone / Fax / Cell:		Email:			
Company/Address:				Urgency:	Low / Medium / High

Date: Time: AM / PM   From:

Message:

Follow up:					Completed: ☐
Phone / Fax / Cell:		Email:			
Company/Address:				Urgency:	Low / Medium / High

Date: Time: AM / PM   From:

Message:

Follow up:					Completed: ☐
Phone / Fax / Cell:		Email:			
Company/Address:				Urgency:	Low / Medium / High

Date: Time: AM / PM   From:

Message:

Follow up:					Completed: ☐
Phone / Fax / Cell:		Email:			
Company/Address:				Urgency:	Low / Medium / High

Date: Time: AM / PM   From:

Message:

Follow up:					Completed: ☐
Phone / Fax / Cell:		Email:			
Company/Address:				Urgency:	Low / Medium / High

Date: Time: AM / PM   From:
Message:
....
....

Follow up:	Completed: ☐
Phone / Fax / Cell: Email:
Company/Address: Urgency: Low / Medium / High

Date: Time: AM / PM   From:
Message:
....
....

Follow up:	Completed: ☐
Phone / Fax / Cell: Email:
Company/Address: Urgency: Low / Medium / High

Date: Time: AM / PM   From:
Message:
....
....

Follow up:	Completed: ☐
Phone / Fax / Cell: Email:
Company/Address: Urgency: Low / Medium / High

Date: Time: AM / PM   From:
Message:
....
....

Follow up:	Completed: ☐
Phone / Fax / Cell: Email:
Company/Address: Urgency: Low / Medium / High

Date: Time: AM / PM   From:
Message:
....
....

Follow up:	Completed: ☐
Phone / Fax / Cell: Email:
Company/Address: Urgency: Low / Medium / High

Date: Time: AM / PM   From:
Message:

Follow up:				Completed: ☐
Phone / Fax / Cell:		Email:		
Company/Address:			Urgency:	Low / Medium / High

Date: Time: AM / PM   From:
Message:

Follow up:				Completed: ☐
Phone / Fax / Cell:		Email:		
Company/Address:			Urgency:	Low / Medium / High

Date: Time: AM / PM   From:
Message:

Follow up:				Completed: ☐
Phone / Fax / Cell:		Email:		
Company/Address:			Urgency:	Low / Medium / High

Date: Time: AM / PM   From:
Message:

Follow up:				Completed: ☐
Phone / Fax / Cell:		Email:		
Company/Address:			Urgency:	Low / Medium / High

Date: Time: AM / PM   From:
Message:

Follow up:				Completed: ☐
Phone / Fax / Cell:		Email:		
Company/Address:			Urgency:	Low / Medium / High

| Date: | Time: | AM / PM | From: |

Message:

Follow up: **Completed:** ☐

Phone / Fax / Cell: Email:
Company/Address: Urgency: Low / Medium / High

| Date: | Time: | AM / PM | From: |

Message:

Follow up: **Completed:** ☐

Phone / Fax / Cell: Email:
Company/Address: Urgency: Low / Medium / High

| Date: | Time: | AM / PM | From: |

Message:

Follow up: **Completed:** ☐

Phone / Fax / Cell: Email:
Company/Address: Urgency: Low / Medium / High

| Date: | Time: | AM / PM | From: |

Message:

Follow up: **Completed:** ☐

Phone / Fax / Cell: Email:
Company/Address: Urgency: Low / Medium / High

| Date: | Time: | AM / PM | From: |

Message:

Follow up: **Completed:** ☐

Phone / Fax / Cell: Email:
Company/Address: Urgency: Low / Medium / High

Date:	Time:	AM / PM	From:

Message:

Follow up:				Completed:	☐
Phone / Fax / Cell:		Email:			
Company/Address:			Urgency:	Low / Medium / High	

Date:	Time:	AM / PM	From:

Message:

Follow up:				Completed:	☐
Phone / Fax / Cell:		Email:			
Company/Address:			Urgency:	Low / Medium / High	

Date:	Time:	AM / PM	From:

Message:

Follow up:				Completed:	☐
Phone / Fax / Cell:		Email:			
Company/Address:			Urgency:	Low / Medium / High	

Date:	Time:	AM / PM	From:

Message:

Follow up:				Completed:	☐
Phone / Fax / Cell:		Email:			
Company/Address:			Urgency:	Low / Medium / High	

Date:	Time:	AM / PM	From:

Message:

Follow up:				Completed:	☐
Phone / Fax / Cell:		Email:			
Company/Address:			Urgency:	Low / Medium / High	

Date: Time: AM / PM   From:
Message:

Follow up: Completed: ☐
Phone / Fax / Cell: Email:
Company/Address: Urgency: Low / Medium / High

Date: Time: AM / PM   From:
Message:

Follow up: Completed: ☐
Phone / Fax / Cell: Email:
Company/Address: Urgency: Low / Medium / High

Date: Time: AM / PM   From:
Message:

Follow up: Completed: ☐
Phone / Fax / Cell: Email:
Company/Address: Urgency: Low / Medium / High

Date: Time: AM / PM   From:
Message:

Follow up: Completed: ☐
Phone / Fax / Cell: Email:
Company/Address: Urgency: Low / Medium / High

Date: Time: AM / PM   From:
Message:

Follow up: Completed: ☐
Phone / Fax / Cell: Email:
Company/Address: Urgency: Low / Medium / High

Date: Time: AM / PM   From:
Message:

Follow up: Completed: ☐
Phone / Fax / Cell: Email:
Company/Address: Urgency: Low / Medium / High

Date: Time: AM / PM   From:
Message:

Follow up: Completed: ☐
Phone / Fax / Cell: Email:
Company/Address: Urgency: Low / Medium / High

Date: Time: AM / PM   From:
Message:

Follow up: Completed: ☐
Phone / Fax / Cell: Email:
Company/Address: Urgency: Low / Medium / High

Date: Time: AM / PM   From:
Message:

Follow up: Completed: ☐
Phone / Fax / Cell: Email:
Company/Address: Urgency: Low / Medium / High

Date: Time: AM / PM   From:
Message:

Follow up: Completed: ☐
Phone / Fax / Cell: Email:
Company/Address: Urgency: Low / Medium / High

Date:	Time:	AM / PM	From:

Message:

Follow up:			Completed: ☐
Phone / Fax / Cell:		Email:	
Company/Address:		Urgency:	Low / Medium / High

Date:	Time:	AM / PM	From:

Message:

Follow up:			Completed: ☐
Phone / Fax / Cell:		Email:	
Company/Address:		Urgency:	Low / Medium / High

Date:	Time:	AM / PM	From:

Message:

Follow up:			Completed: ☐
Phone / Fax / Cell:		Email:	
Company/Address:		Urgency:	Low / Medium / High

Date:	Time:	AM / PM	From:

Message:

Follow up:			Completed: ☐
Phone / Fax / Cell:		Email:	
Company/Address:		Urgency:	Low / Medium / High

Date:	Time:	AM / PM	From:

Message:

Follow up:			Completed: ☐
Phone / Fax / Cell:		Email:	
Company/Address:		Urgency:	Low / Medium / High

Date: Time: AM / PM   From:

Message:

Follow up:				Completed: ☐
Phone / Fax / Cell:		Email:		
Company/Address:			Urgency:	Low / Medium / High

Date: Time: AM / PM   From:

Message:

Follow up:				Completed: ☐
Phone / Fax / Cell:		Email:		
Company/Address:			Urgency:	Low / Medium / High

Date: Time: AM / PM   From:

Message:

Follow up:				Completed: ☐
Phone / Fax / Cell:		Email:		
Company/Address:			Urgency:	Low / Medium / High

Date: Time: AM / PM   From:

Message:

Follow up:				Completed: ☐
Phone / Fax / Cell:		Email:		
Company/Address:			Urgency:	Low / Medium / High

Date: Time: AM / PM   From:

Message:

Follow up:				Completed: ☐
Phone / Fax / Cell:		Email:		
Company/Address:			Urgency:	Low / Medium / High

| Date: | Time: | AM / PM | From: |

Message:

Follow up: **Completed:** ☐

Phone / Fax / Cell: Email:
Company/Address: Urgency: Low / Medium / High

| Date: | Time: | AM / PM | From: |

Message:

Follow up: **Completed:** ☐

Phone / Fax / Cell: Email:
Company/Address: Urgency: Low / Medium / High

| Date: | Time: | AM / PM | From: |

Message:

Follow up: **Completed:** ☐

Phone / Fax / Cell: Email:
Company/Address: Urgency: Low / Medium / High

| Date: | Time: | AM / PM | From: |

Message:

Follow up: **Completed:** ☐

Phone / Fax / Cell: Email:
Company/Address: Urgency: Low / Medium / High

| Date: | Time: | AM / PM | From: |

Message:

Follow up: **Completed:** ☐

Phone / Fax / Cell: Email:
Company/Address: Urgency: Low / Medium / High

Date:　　　　　　　　Time:　　　　　　　　AM / PM　From:

Message:

Follow up:		Completed: ☐
Phone / Fax / Cell:	Email:	
Company/Address:	Urgency:	Low / Medium / High

Date:　　　　　　　　Time:　　　　　　　　AM / PM　From:

Message:

Follow up:		Completed: ☐
Phone / Fax / Cell:	Email:	
Company/Address:	Urgency:	Low / Medium / High

Date:　　　　　　　　Time:　　　　　　　　AM / PM　From:

Message:

Follow up:		Completed: ☐
Phone / Fax / Cell:	Email:	
Company/Address:	Urgency:	Low / Medium / High

Date:　　　　　　　　Time:　　　　　　　　AM / PM　From:

Message:

Follow up:		Completed: ☐
Phone / Fax / Cell:	Email:	
Company/Address:	Urgency:	Low / Medium / High

Date:　　　　　　　　Time:　　　　　　　　AM / PM　From:

Message:

Follow up:		Completed: ☐
Phone / Fax / Cell:	Email:	
Company/Address:	Urgency:	Low / Medium / High

Date: Time: AM / PM   From:
Message:

Follow up: **Completed:**
Phone / Fax / Cell: Email:
Company/Address: Urgency: Low / Medium / High

Date: Time: AM / PM   From:
Message:

Follow up: **Completed:**
Phone / Fax / Cell: Email:
Company/Address: Urgency: Low / Medium / High

Date: Time: AM / PM   From:
Message:

Follow up: **Completed:**
Phone / Fax / Cell: Email:
Company/Address: Urgency: Low / Medium / High

Date: Time: AM / PM   From:
Message:

Follow up: **Completed:**
Phone / Fax / Cell: Email:
Company/Address: Urgency: Low / Medium / High

Date: Time: AM / PM   From:
Message:

Follow up: **Completed:**
Phone / Fax / Cell: Email:
Company/Address: Urgency: Low / Medium / High

Date: Time: AM / PM   From:
Message:

Follow up:			Completed:	☐
Phone / Fax / Cell:		Email:		
Company/Address:			Urgency: Low / Medium / High	

Date: Time: AM / PM   From:
Message:

Follow up:			Completed:	☐
Phone / Fax / Cell:		Email:		
Company/Address:			Urgency: Low / Medium / High	

Date: Time: AM / PM   From:
Message:

Follow up:			Completed:	☐
Phone / Fax / Cell:		Email:		
Company/Address:			Urgency: Low / Medium / High	

Date: Time: AM / PM   From:
Message:

Follow up:			Completed:	☐
Phone / Fax / Cell:		Email:		
Company/Address:			Urgency: Low / Medium / High	

Date: Time: AM / PM   From:
Message:

Follow up:			Completed:	☐
Phone / Fax / Cell:		Email:		
Company/Address:			Urgency: Low / Medium / High	

Date:	Time:	AM / PM	From:

Message:

Follow up: **Completed:** ☐

Phone / Fax / Cell: Email:

Company/Address: Urgency: Low / Medium / High

Date:	Time:	AM / PM	From:

Message:

Follow up: **Completed:** ☐

Phone / Fax / Cell: Email:

Company/Address: Urgency: Low / Medium / High

Date:	Time:	AM / PM	From:

Message:

Follow up: **Completed:** ☐

Phone / Fax / Cell: Email:

Company/Address: Urgency: Low / Medium / High

Date:	Time:	AM / PM	From:

Message:

Follow up: **Completed:** ☐

Phone / Fax / Cell: Email:

Company/Address: Urgency: Low / Medium / High

Date:	Time:	AM / PM	From:

Message:

Follow up: **Completed:** ☐

Phone / Fax / Cell: Email:

Company/Address: Urgency: Low / Medium / High

Date: Time: AM / PM   From:
Message:

Follow up: Completed: ☐
Phone / Fax / Cell: Email:
Company/Address: Urgency: Low / Medium / High

Date: Time: AM / PM   From:
Message:

Follow up: Completed: ☐
Phone / Fax / Cell: Email:
Company/Address: Urgency: Low / Medium / High

Date: Time: AM / PM   From:
Message:

Follow up: Completed: ☐
Phone / Fax / Cell: Email:
Company/Address: Urgency: Low / Medium / High

Date: Time: AM / PM   From:
Message:

Follow up: Completed: ☐
Phone / Fax / Cell: Email:
Company/Address: Urgency: Low / Medium / High

Date: Time: AM / PM   From:
Message:

Follow up: Completed: ☐
Phone / Fax / Cell: Email:
Company/Address: Urgency: Low / Medium / High

Date: Time: AM / PM   From:

Message:

....

Follow up:	Completed: ☐

Phone / Fax / Cell: Email:

Company/Address: Urgency: Low / Medium / High

Date: Time: AM / PM   From:

Message:

....

Follow up:	Completed: ☐

Phone / Fax / Cell: Email:

Company/Address: Urgency: Low / Medium / High

Date: Time: AM / PM   From:

Message:

....

Follow up:	Completed: ☐

Phone / Fax / Cell: Email:

Company/Address: Urgency: Low / Medium / High

Date: Time: AM / PM   From:

Message:

....

Follow up:	Completed: ☐

Phone / Fax / Cell: Email:

Company/Address: Urgency: Low / Medium / High

Date: Time: AM / PM   From:

Message:

....

Follow up:	Completed: ☐

Phone / Fax / Cell: Email:

Company/Address: Urgency: Low / Medium / High

Date: Time: AM / PM   From:

Message:

Follow up: Completed: ☐

Phone / Fax / Cell: Email:

Company/Address: Urgency: Low / Medium / High

Date: Time: AM / PM   From:

Message:

Follow up: Completed: ☐

Phone / Fax / Cell: Email:

Company/Address: Urgency: Low / Medium / High

Date: Time: AM / PM   From:

Message:

Follow up: Completed: ☐

Phone / Fax / Cell: Email:

Company/Address: Urgency: Low / Medium / High

Date: Time: AM / PM   From:

Message:

Follow up: Completed: ☐

Phone / Fax / Cell: Email:

Company/Address: Urgency: Low / Medium / High

Date: Time: AM / PM   From:

Message:

Follow up: Completed: ☐

Phone / Fax / Cell: Email:

Company/Address: Urgency: Low / Medium / High

Date: Time: AM / PM   From:
Message:
....
....

Follow up:			Completed:	☐
Phone / Fax / Cell:		Email:		
Company/Address:			Urgency: Low / Medium / High	

Date: Time: AM / PM   From:
Message:
....
....

Follow up:			Completed:	☐
Phone / Fax / Cell:		Email:		
Company/Address:			Urgency: Low / Medium / High	

Date: Time: AM / PM   From:
Message:
....
....

Follow up:			Completed:	☐
Phone / Fax / Cell:		Email:		
Company/Address:			Urgency: Low / Medium / High	

Date: Time: AM / PM   From:
Message:
....
....

Follow up:			Completed:	☐
Phone / Fax / Cell:		Email:		
Company/Address:			Urgency: Low / Medium / High	

Date: Time: AM / PM   From:
Message:
....
....

Follow up:			Completed:	☐
Phone / Fax / Cell:		Email:		
Company/Address:			Urgency: Low / Medium / High	

Date: Time: AM / PM   From:

Message:

Follow up: **Completed:** ☐

Phone / Fax / Cell: Email:

Company/Address: Urgency: Low / Medium / High

Date: Time: AM / PM   From:

Message:

Follow up: **Completed:** ☐

Phone / Fax / Cell: Email:

Company/Address: Urgency: Low / Medium / High

Date: Time: AM / PM   From:

Message:

Follow up: **Completed:** ☐

Phone / Fax / Cell: Email:

Company/Address: Urgency: Low / Medium / High

Date: Time: AM / PM   From:

Message:

Follow up: **Completed:** ☐

Phone / Fax / Cell: Email:

Company/Address: Urgency: Low / Medium / High

Date: Time: AM / PM   From:

Message:

Follow up: **Completed:** ☐

Phone / Fax / Cell: Email:

Company/Address: Urgency: Low / Medium / High

Date: Time: AM / PM   From:

Message:

Follow up: Completed: ☐

Phone / Fax / Cell: Email:

Company/Address: Urgency: Low / Medium / High

Date: Time: AM / PM   From:

Message:

Follow up: Completed: ☐

Phone / Fax / Cell: Email:

Company/Address: Urgency: Low / Medium / High

Date: Time: AM / PM   From:

Message:

Follow up: Completed: ☐

Phone / Fax / Cell: Email:

Company/Address: Urgency: Low / Medium / High

Date: Time: AM / PM   From:

Message:

Follow up: Completed: ☐

Phone / Fax / Cell: Email:

Company/Address: Urgency: Low / Medium / High

Date: Time: AM / PM   From:

Message:

Follow up: Completed: ☐

Phone / Fax / Cell: Email:

Company/Address: Urgency: Low / Medium / High

Date: Time: AM / PM   From:
Message:

Follow up: Completed: ☐
Phone / Fax / Cell: Email:
Company/Address: Urgency: Low / Medium / High

Date: Time: AM / PM   From:
Message:

Follow up: Completed: ☐
Phone / Fax / Cell: Email:
Company/Address: Urgency: Low / Medium / High

Date: Time: AM / PM   From:
Message:

Follow up: Completed: ☐
Phone / Fax / Cell: Email:
Company/Address: Urgency: Low / Medium / High

Date: Time: AM / PM   From:
Message:

Follow up: Completed: ☐
Phone / Fax / Cell: Email:
Company/Address: Urgency: Low / Medium / High

Date: Time: AM / PM   From:
Message:

Follow up: Completed: ☐
Phone / Fax / Cell: Email:
Company/Address: Urgency: Low / Medium / High

Date:	Time:	AM / PM	From:

Message:

Follow up: Completed: ☐

Phone / Fax / Cell: Email:

Company/Address: Urgency: Low / Medium / High

Date:	Time:	AM / PM	From:

Message:

Follow up: Completed: ☐

Phone / Fax / Cell: Email:

Company/Address: Urgency: Low / Medium / High

Date:	Time:	AM / PM	From:

Message:

Follow up: Completed: ☐

Phone / Fax / Cell: Email:

Company/Address: Urgency: Low / Medium / High

Date:	Time:	AM / PM	From:

Message:

Follow up: Completed: ☐

Phone / Fax / Cell: Email:

Company/Address: Urgency: Low / Medium / High

Date:	Time:	AM / PM	From:

Message:

Follow up: Completed: ☐

Phone / Fax / Cell: Email:

Company/Address: Urgency: Low / Medium / High

Date: Time: AM / PM   From:
Message:

Follow up:	Completed: ☐

Phone / Fax / Cell: Email:
Company/Address: Urgency: Low / Medium / High

Date: Time: AM / PM   From:
Message:

Follow up:	Completed: ☐

Phone / Fax / Cell: Email:
Company/Address: Urgency: Low / Medium / High

Date: Time: AM / PM   From:
Message:

Follow up:	Completed: ☐

Phone / Fax / Cell: Email:
Company/Address: Urgency: Low / Medium / High

Date: Time: AM / PM   From:
Message:

Follow up:	Completed: ☐

Phone / Fax / Cell: Email:
Company/Address: Urgency: Low / Medium / High

Date: Time: AM / PM   From:
Message:

Follow up:	Completed: ☐

Phone / Fax / Cell: Email:
Company/Address: Urgency: Low / Medium / High

| Date: | Time: | AM / PM | From: |

Message:

Follow up: Completed: ☐

Phone / Fax / Cell: Email:
Company/Address: Urgency: Low / Medium / High

| Date: | Time: | AM / PM | From: |

Message:

Follow up: Completed: ☐

Phone / Fax / Cell: Email:
Company/Address: Urgency: Low / Medium / High

| Date: | Time: | AM / PM | From: |

Message:

Follow up: Completed: ☐

Phone / Fax / Cell: Email:
Company/Address: Urgency: Low / Medium / High

| Date: | Time: | AM / PM | From: |

Message:

Follow up: Completed: ☐

Phone / Fax / Cell: Email:
Company/Address: Urgency: Low / Medium / High

| Date: | Time: | AM / PM | From: |

Message:

Follow up: Completed: ☐

Phone / Fax / Cell: Email:
Company/Address: Urgency: Low / Medium / High

Date: Time: AM / PM From:
Message:

Follow up: Completed: ☐
Phone / Fax / Cell: Email:
Company/Address: Urgency: Low / Medium / High

Date: Time: AM / PM From:
Message:

Follow up: Completed: ☐
Phone / Fax / Cell: Email:
Company/Address: Urgency: Low / Medium / High

Date: Time: AM / PM From:
Message:

Follow up: Completed: ☐
Phone / Fax / Cell: Email:
Company/Address: Urgency: Low / Medium / High

Date: Time: AM / PM From:
Message:

Follow up: Completed: ☐
Phone / Fax / Cell: Email:
Company/Address: Urgency: Low / Medium / High

Date: Time: AM / PM From:
Message:

Follow up: Completed: ☐
Phone / Fax / Cell: Email:
Company/Address: Urgency: Low / Medium / High

Date: Time: AM / PM   From:
Message:

Follow up: **Completed:**
Phone / Fax / Cell: Email:
Company/Address: Urgency: Low / Medium / High

Date: Time: AM / PM   From:
Message:

Follow up: **Completed:**
Phone / Fax / Cell: Email:
Company/Address: Urgency: Low / Medium / High

Date: Time: AM / PM   From:
Message:

Follow up: **Completed:**
Phone / Fax / Cell: Email:
Company/Address: Urgency: Low / Medium / High

Date: Time: AM / PM   From:
Message:

Follow up: **Completed:**
Phone / Fax / Cell: Email:
Company/Address: Urgency: Low / Medium / High

Date: Time: AM / PM   From:
Message:

Follow up: **Completed:**
Phone / Fax / Cell: Email:
Company/Address: Urgency: Low / Medium / High

Date: Time: AM / PM   From:
Message:

Follow up:			Completed:	☐
Phone / Fax / Cell: Email:
Company/Address: Urgency: Low / Medium / High

Date: Time: AM / PM   From:
Message:

Follow up:			Completed:	☐
Phone / Fax / Cell: Email:
Company/Address: Urgency: Low / Medium / High

Date: Time: AM / PM   From:
Message:

Follow up:			Completed:	☐
Phone / Fax / Cell: Email:
Company/Address: Urgency: Low / Medium / High

Date: Time: AM / PM   From:
Message:

Follow up:			Completed:	☐
Phone / Fax / Cell: Email:
Company/Address: Urgency: Low / Medium / High

Date: Time: AM / PM   From:
Message:

Follow up:			Completed:	☐
Phone / Fax / Cell: Email:
Company/Address: Urgency: Low / Medium / High

Date: Time: AM / PM From:

Message:

Follow up: Completed: ☐

Phone / Fax / Cell: Email:

Company/Address: Urgency: Low / Medium / High

Date: Time: AM / PM From:

Message:

Follow up: Completed: ☐

Phone / Fax / Cell: Email:

Company/Address: Urgency: Low / Medium / High

Date: Time: AM / PM From:

Message:

Follow up: Completed: ☐

Phone / Fax / Cell: Email:

Company/Address: Urgency: Low / Medium / High

Date: Time: AM / PM From:

Message:

Follow up: Completed: ☐

Phone / Fax / Cell: Email:

Company/Address: Urgency: Low / Medium / High

Date: Time: AM / PM From:

Message:

Follow up: Completed: ☐

Phone / Fax / Cell: Email:

Company/Address: Urgency: Low / Medium / High

Date: Time: AM / PM   From:

Message:

Follow up:			Completed: ☐
Phone / Fax / Cell:		Email:	
Company/Address:		Urgency:	Low / Medium / High

Date: Time: AM / PM   From:

Message:

Follow up:			Completed: ☐
Phone / Fax / Cell:		Email:	
Company/Address:		Urgency:	Low / Medium / High

Date: Time: AM / PM   From:

Message:

Follow up:			Completed: ☐
Phone / Fax / Cell:		Email:	
Company/Address:		Urgency:	Low / Medium / High

Date: Time: AM / PM   From:

Message:

Follow up:			Completed: ☐
Phone / Fax / Cell:		Email:	
Company/Address:		Urgency:	Low / Medium / High

Date: Time: AM / PM   From:

Message:

Follow up:			Completed: ☐
Phone / Fax / Cell:		Email:	
Company/Address:		Urgency:	Low / Medium / High

| Date: | Time: | AM / PM | From: |

Message:

Follow up: Completed: ☐

Phone / Fax / Cell: Email:

Company/Address: Urgency: Low / Medium / High

| Date: | Time: | AM / PM | From: |

Message:

Follow up: Completed: ☐

Phone / Fax / Cell: Email:

Company/Address: Urgency: Low / Medium / High

| Date: | Time: | AM / PM | From: |

Message:

Follow up: Completed: ☐

Phone / Fax / Cell: Email:

Company/Address: Urgency: Low / Medium / High

| Date: | Time: | AM / PM | From: |

Message:

Follow up: Completed: ☐

Phone / Fax / Cell: Email:

Company/Address: Urgency: Low / Medium / High

| Date: | Time: | AM / PM | From: |

Message:

Follow up: Completed: ☐

Phone / Fax / Cell: Email:

Company/Address: Urgency: Low / Medium / High

Date: Time: AM / PM From:
Message:

Follow up:	Completed: ☐

Phone / Fax / Cell: Email:
Company/Address: Urgency: Low / Medium / High

Date: Time: AM / PM From:
Message:

Follow up:	Completed: ☐

Phone / Fax / Cell: Email:
Company/Address: Urgency: Low / Medium / High

Date: Time: AM / PM From:
Message:

Follow up:	Completed: ☐

Phone / Fax / Cell: Email:
Company/Address: Urgency: Low / Medium / High

Date: Time: AM / PM From:
Message:

Follow up:	Completed: ☐

Phone / Fax / Cell: Email:
Company/Address: Urgency: Low / Medium / High

Date: Time: AM / PM From:
Message:

Follow up:	Completed: ☐

Phone / Fax / Cell: Email:
Company/Address: Urgency: Low / Medium / High

Date: Time: AM / PM   From:
Message:

| Follow up: | | | Completed: ☐ |
Phone / Fax / Cell: Email:
Company/Address: Urgency: Low / Medium / High

Date: Time: AM / PM   From:
Message:

| Follow up: | | | Completed: ☐ |
Phone / Fax / Cell: Email:
Company/Address: Urgency: Low / Medium / High

Date: Time: AM / PM   From:
Message:

| Follow up: | | | Completed: ☐ |
Phone / Fax / Cell: Email:
Company/Address: Urgency: Low / Medium / High

Date: Time: AM / PM   From:
Message:

| Follow up: | | | Completed: ☐ |
Phone / Fax / Cell: Email:
Company/Address: Urgency: Low / Medium / High

Date: Time: AM / PM   From:
Message:

| Follow up: | | | Completed: ☐ |
Phone / Fax / Cell: Email:
Company/Address: Urgency: Low / Medium / High

Date: Time: AM / PM   From:
Message:

Follow up: Completed: ☐
Phone / Fax / Cell: Email:
Company/Address: Urgency: Low / Medium / High

Date: Time: AM / PM   From:
Message:

Follow up: Completed: ☐
Phone / Fax / Cell: Email:
Company/Address: Urgency: Low / Medium / High

Date: Time: AM / PM   From:
Message:

Follow up: Completed: ☐
Phone / Fax / Cell: Email:
Company/Address: Urgency: Low / Medium / High

Date: Time: AM / PM   From:
Message:

Follow up: Completed: ☐
Phone / Fax / Cell: Email:
Company/Address: Urgency: Low / Medium / High

Date: Time: AM / PM   From:
Message:

Follow up: Completed: ☐
Phone / Fax / Cell: Email:
Company/Address: Urgency: Low / Medium / High

Date: Time: AM / PM   From:

Message:

Follow up: **Completed:**

Phone / Fax / Cell: Email:

Company/Address: Urgency: Low / Medium / High

Date: Time: AM / PM   From:

Message:

Follow up: **Completed:**

Phone / Fax / Cell: Email:

Company/Address: Urgency: Low / Medium / High

Date: Time: AM / PM   From:

Message:

Follow up: **Completed:**

Phone / Fax / Cell: Email:

Company/Address: Urgency: Low / Medium / High

Date: Time: AM / PM   From:

Message:

Follow up: **Completed:**

Phone / Fax / Cell: Email:

Company/Address: Urgency: Low / Medium / High

Date: Time: AM / PM   From:

Message:

Follow up: **Completed:**

Phone / Fax / Cell: Email:

Company/Address: Urgency: Low / Medium / High

| Date: | Time: | AM / PM | From: |

Message:

Follow up: Completed: ☐

Phone / Fax / Cell: Email:

Company/Address: Urgency: Low / Medium / High

| Date: | Time: | AM / PM | From: |

Message:

Follow up: Completed: ☐

Phone / Fax / Cell: Email:

Company/Address: Urgency: Low / Medium / High

| Date: | Time: | AM / PM | From: |

Message:

Follow up: Completed: ☐

Phone / Fax / Cell: Email:

Company/Address: Urgency: Low / Medium / High

| Date: | Time: | AM / PM | From: |

Message:

Follow up: Completed: ☐

Phone / Fax / Cell: Email:

Company/Address: Urgency: Low / Medium / High

| Date: | Time: | AM / PM | From: |

Message:

Follow up: Completed: ☐

Phone / Fax / Cell: Email:

Company/Address: Urgency: Low / Medium / High

| Date: | Time: | AM / PM | From: |

Message:

Follow up: Completed: ☐

Phone / Fax / Cell: Email:
Company/Address: Urgency: Low / Medium / High

| Date: | Time: | AM / PM | From: |

Message:

Follow up: Completed: ☐

Phone / Fax / Cell: Email:
Company/Address: Urgency: Low / Medium / High

| Date: | Time: | AM / PM | From: |

Message:

Follow up: Completed: ☐

Phone / Fax / Cell: Email:
Company/Address: Urgency: Low / Medium / High

| Date: | Time: | AM / PM | From: |

Message:

Follow up: Completed: ☐

Phone / Fax / Cell: Email:
Company/Address: Urgency: Low / Medium / High

| Date: | Time: | AM / PM | From: |

Message:

Follow up: Completed: ☐

Phone / Fax / Cell: Email:
Company/Address: Urgency: Low / Medium / High

Date: Time: AM / PM   From:
Message:

| Follow up: | | | Completed: | ☐ |

Phone / Fax / Cell: Email:
Company/Address: Urgency: Low / Medium / High

Date: Time: AM / PM   From:
Message:

| Follow up: | | | Completed: | ☐ |

Phone / Fax / Cell: Email:
Company/Address: Urgency: Low / Medium / High

Date: Time: AM / PM   From:
Message:

| Follow up: | | | Completed: | ☐ |

Phone / Fax / Cell: Email:
Company/Address: Urgency: Low / Medium / High

Date: Time: AM / PM   From:
Message:

| Follow up: | | | Completed: | ☐ |

Phone / Fax / Cell: Email:
Company/Address: Urgency: Low / Medium / High

Date: Time: AM / PM   From:
Message:

| Follow up: | | | Completed: | ☐ |

Phone / Fax / Cell: Email:
Company/Address: Urgency: Low / Medium / High

Date: Time: AM / PM   From:
Message:

| Follow up: | | | | Completed: | ☐ |

Phone / Fax / Cell: Email:
Company/Address: Urgency: Low / Medium / High

Date: Time: AM / PM   From:
Message:

| Follow up: | | | | Completed: | ☐ |

Phone / Fax / Cell: Email:
Company/Address: Urgency: Low / Medium / High

Date: Time: AM / PM   From:
Message:

| Follow up: | | | | Completed: | ☐ |

Phone / Fax / Cell: Email:
Company/Address: Urgency: Low / Medium / High

Date: Time: AM / PM   From:
Message:

| Follow up: | | | | Completed: | ☐ |

Phone / Fax / Cell: Email:
Company/Address: Urgency: Low / Medium / High

Date: Time: AM / PM   From:
Message:

| Follow up: | | | | Completed: | ☐ |

Phone / Fax / Cell: Email:
Company/Address: Urgency: Low / Medium / High

Date: Time: AM / PM   From:
Message:

Follow up:			Completed: ☐
Phone / Fax / Cell:		Email:	
Company/Address:		Urgency:	Low / Medium / High

Date: Time: AM / PM   From:
Message:

Follow up:			Completed: ☐
Phone / Fax / Cell:		Email:	
Company/Address:		Urgency:	Low / Medium / High

Date: Time: AM / PM   From:
Message:

Follow up:			Completed: ☐
Phone / Fax / Cell:		Email:	
Company/Address:		Urgency:	Low / Medium / High

Date: Time: AM / PM   From:
Message:

Follow up:			Completed: ☐
Phone / Fax / Cell:		Email:	
Company/Address:		Urgency:	Low / Medium / High

Date: Time: AM / PM   From:
Message:

Follow up:			Completed: ☐
Phone / Fax / Cell:		Email:	
Company/Address:		Urgency:	Low / Medium / High

Date: Time: AM / PM   From:
Message:

Follow up: **Completed:**
Phone / Fax / Cell: Email:
Company/Address: Urgency: Low / Medium / High

Date: Time: AM / PM   From:
Message:

Follow up: **Completed:**
Phone / Fax / Cell: Email:
Company/Address: Urgency: Low / Medium / High

Date: Time: AM / PM   From:
Message:

Follow up: **Completed:**
Phone / Fax / Cell: Email:
Company/Address: Urgency: Low / Medium / High

Date: Time: AM / PM   From:
Message:

Follow up: **Completed:**
Phone / Fax / Cell: Email:
Company/Address: Urgency: Low / Medium / High

Date: Time: AM / PM   From:
Message:

Follow up: **Completed:**
Phone / Fax / Cell: Email:
Company/Address: Urgency: Low / Medium / High

Date: Time: AM / PM   From:

Message:

....

Follow up:		Completed: ☐

Phone / Fax / Cell: Email:

Company/Address: Urgency: Low / Medium / High

Date: Time: AM / PM   From:

Message:

....

Follow up:		Completed: ☐

Phone / Fax / Cell: Email:

Company/Address: Urgency: Low / Medium / High

Date: Time: AM / PM   From:

Message:

....

Follow up:		Completed: ☐

Phone / Fax / Cell: Email:

Company/Address: Urgency: Low / Medium / High

Date: Time: AM / PM   From:

Message:

....

Follow up:		Completed: ☐

Phone / Fax / Cell: Email:

Company/Address: Urgency: Low / Medium / High

Date: Time: AM / PM   From:

Message:

....

Follow up:		Completed: ☐

Phone / Fax / Cell: Email:

Company/Address: Urgency: Low / Medium / High

Date: Time: AM / PM   From:
Message:

Follow up:			Completed: ☐
Phone / Fax / Cell:		Email:	
Company/Address:		Urgency:	Low / Medium / High

Date: Time: AM / PM   From:
Message:

Follow up:			Completed: ☐
Phone / Fax / Cell:		Email:	
Company/Address:		Urgency:	Low / Medium / High

Date: Time: AM / PM   From:
Message:

Follow up:			Completed: ☐
Phone / Fax / Cell:		Email:	
Company/Address:		Urgency:	Low / Medium / High

Date: Time: AM / PM   From:
Message:

Follow up:			Completed: ☐
Phone / Fax / Cell:		Email:	
Company/Address:		Urgency:	Low / Medium / High

Date: Time: AM / PM   From:
Message:

Follow up:			Completed: ☐
Phone / Fax / Cell:		Email:	
Company/Address:		Urgency:	Low / Medium / High

Date: Time: AM / PM   From:
Message:

Follow up: Completed: ☐
Phone / Fax / Cell: Email:
Company/Address: Urgency: Low / Medium / High

Date: Time: AM / PM   From:
Message:

Follow up: Completed: ☐
Phone / Fax / Cell: Email:
Company/Address: Urgency: Low / Medium / High

Date: Time: AM / PM   From:
Message:

Follow up: Completed: ☐
Phone / Fax / Cell: Email:
Company/Address: Urgency: Low / Medium / High

Date: Time: AM / PM   From:
Message:

Follow up: Completed: ☐
Phone / Fax / Cell: Email:
Company/Address: Urgency: Low / Medium / High

Date: Time: AM / PM   From:
Message:

Follow up: Completed: ☐
Phone / Fax / Cell: Email:
Company/Address: Urgency: Low / Medium / High

Date: Time: AM / PM   From:
Message:
....

Follow up:			Completed: ☐
Phone / Fax / Cell:		Email:	
Company/Address:		Urgency:	Low / Medium / High

Date: Time: AM / PM   From:
Message:
....

Follow up:			Completed: ☐
Phone / Fax / Cell:		Email:	
Company/Address:		Urgency:	Low / Medium / High

Date: Time: AM / PM   From:
Message:
....

Follow up:			Completed: ☐
Phone / Fax / Cell:		Email:	
Company/Address:		Urgency:	Low / Medium / High

Date: Time: AM / PM   From:
Message:
....

Follow up:			Completed: ☐
Phone / Fax / Cell:		Email:	
Company/Address:		Urgency:	Low / Medium / High

Date: Time: AM / PM   From:
Message:
....

Follow up:			Completed: ☐
Phone / Fax / Cell:		Email:	
Company/Address:		Urgency:	Low / Medium / High

Date:	Time:	AM / PM	From:
Message:

Follow up:				Completed: ☐
Phone / Fax / Cell:		Email:		
Company/Address:			Urgency:	Low / Medium / High

Date:	Time:	AM / PM	From:
Message:

Follow up:				Completed: ☐
Phone / Fax / Cell:		Email:		
Company/Address:			Urgency:	Low / Medium / High

Date:	Time:	AM / PM	From:
Message:

Follow up:				Completed: ☐
Phone / Fax / Cell:		Email:		
Company/Address:			Urgency:	Low / Medium / High

Date:	Time:	AM / PM	From:
Message:

Follow up:				Completed: ☐
Phone / Fax / Cell:		Email:		
Company/Address:			Urgency:	Low / Medium / High

Date:	Time:	AM / PM	From:
Message:

Follow up:				Completed: ☐
Phone / Fax / Cell:		Email:		
Company/Address:			Urgency:	Low / Medium / High

Date:　　　　　　　　Time:　　　　　　AM / PM　From:

Message:

Follow up:　　　　　　　　　　　　　　　　　　　　　**Completed:** ☐

Phone / Fax / Cell:　　　　　　　　　Email:

Company/Address:　　　　　　　　　　　　　Urgency:　Low / Medium / High

Date:　　　　　　　　Time:　　　　　　AM / PM　From:

Message:

Follow up:　　　　　　　　　　　　　　　　　　　　　**Completed:** ☐

Phone / Fax / Cell:　　　　　　　　　Email:

Company/Address:　　　　　　　　　　　　　Urgency:　Low / Medium / High

Date:　　　　　　　　Time:　　　　　　AM / PM　From:

Message:

Follow up:　　　　　　　　　　　　　　　　　　　　　**Completed:** ☐

Phone / Fax / Cell:　　　　　　　　　Email:

Company/Address:　　　　　　　　　　　　　Urgency:　Low / Medium / High

Date:　　　　　　　　Time:　　　　　　AM / PM　From:

Message:

Follow up:　　　　　　　　　　　　　　　　　　　　　**Completed:** ☐

Phone / Fax / Cell:　　　　　　　　　Email:

Company/Address:　　　　　　　　　　　　　Urgency:　Low / Medium / High

Date:　　　　　　　　Time:　　　　　　AM / PM　From:

Message:

Follow up:　　　　　　　　　　　　　　　　　　　　　**Completed:** ☐

Phone / Fax / Cell:　　　　　　　　　Email:

Company/Address:　　　　　　　　　　　　　Urgency:　Low / Medium / High

Date:　　　　　　　Time:　　　　　　　AM / PM　From:
Message:

Follow up:				Completed: ☐
Phone / Fax / Cell:		Email:		
Company/Address:			Urgency:	Low / Medium / High

Date:　　　　　　　Time:　　　　　　　AM / PM　From:
Message:

Follow up:				Completed: ☐
Phone / Fax / Cell:		Email:		
Company/Address:			Urgency:	Low / Medium / High

Date:　　　　　　　Time:　　　　　　　AM / PM　From:
Message:

Follow up:				Completed: ☐
Phone / Fax / Cell:		Email:		
Company/Address:			Urgency:	Low / Medium / High

Date:　　　　　　　Time:　　　　　　　AM / PM　From:
Message:

Follow up:				Completed: ☐
Phone / Fax / Cell:		Email:		
Company/Address:			Urgency:	Low / Medium / High

Date:　　　　　　　Time:　　　　　　　AM / PM　From:
Message:

Follow up:				Completed: ☐
Phone / Fax / Cell:		Email:		
Company/Address:			Urgency:	Low / Medium / High

Date:　　　　　　　Time:　　　　　　AM / PM　From:

Message:

Follow up:　　　　　　　　　　　　　　　　　　　　Completed: ☐

Phone / Fax / Cell:　　　　　　　　　Email:

Company/Address:　　　　　　　　　　　　Urgency:　Low / Medium / High

Date:　　　　　　　Time:　　　　　　AM / PM　From:

Message:

Follow up:　　　　　　　　　　　　　　　　　　　　Completed: ☐

Phone / Fax / Cell:　　　　　　　　　Email:

Company/Address:　　　　　　　　　　　　Urgency:　Low / Medium / High

Date:　　　　　　　Time:　　　　　　AM / PM　From:

Message:

Follow up:　　　　　　　　　　　　　　　　　　　　Completed: ☐

Phone / Fax / Cell:　　　　　　　　　Email:

Company/Address:　　　　　　　　　　　　Urgency:　Low / Medium / High

Date:　　　　　　　Time:　　　　　　AM / PM　From:

Message:

Follow up:　　　　　　　　　　　　　　　　　　　　Completed: ☐

Phone / Fax / Cell:　　　　　　　　　Email:

Company/Address:　　　　　　　　　　　　Urgency:　Low / Medium / High

Date:　　　　　　　Time:　　　　　　AM / PM　From:

Message:

Follow up:　　　　　　　　　　　　　　　　　　　　Completed: ☐

Phone / Fax / Cell:　　　　　　　　　Email:

Company/Address:　　　　　　　　　　　　Urgency:　Low / Medium / High

Date:　　　　　　　Time:　　　　　　　AM / PM　From:

Message:

Follow up:　　　　　　　　　　　　　　　　　　　　　　Completed: ☐

Phone / Fax / Cell:　　　　　　　　　　Email:

Company/Address:　　　　　　　　　　　　　Urgency:　Low / Medium / High

Date:　　　　　　　Time:　　　　　　　AM / PM　From:

Message:

Follow up:　　　　　　　　　　　　　　　　　　　　　　Completed: ☐

Phone / Fax / Cell:　　　　　　　　　　Email:

Company/Address:　　　　　　　　　　　　　Urgency:　Low / Medium / High

Date:　　　　　　　Time:　　　　　　　AM / PM　From:

Message:

Follow up:　　　　　　　　　　　　　　　　　　　　　　Completed: ☐

Phone / Fax / Cell:　　　　　　　　　　Email:

Company/Address:　　　　　　　　　　　　　Urgency:　Low / Medium / High

Date:　　　　　　　Time:　　　　　　　AM / PM　From:

Message:

Follow up:　　　　　　　　　　　　　　　　　　　　　　Completed: ☐

Phone / Fax / Cell:　　　　　　　　　　Email:

Company/Address:　　　　　　　　　　　　　Urgency:　Low / Medium / High

Date:　　　　　　　Time:　　　　　　　AM / PM　From:

Message:

Follow up:　　　　　　　　　　　　　　　　　　　　　　Completed: ☐

Phone / Fax / Cell:　　　　　　　　　　Email:

Company/Address:　　　　　　　　　　　　　Urgency:　Low / Medium / High

Date:	Time:	AM / PM	From:

Message:

Follow up: Completed: ☐

Phone / Fax / Cell: Email:

Company/Address: Urgency: Low / Medium / High

Date:	Time:	AM / PM	From:

Message:

Follow up: Completed: ☐

Phone / Fax / Cell: Email:

Company/Address: Urgency: Low / Medium / High

Date:	Time:	AM / PM	From:

Message:

Follow up: Completed: ☐

Phone / Fax / Cell: Email:

Company/Address: Urgency: Low / Medium / High

Date:	Time:	AM / PM	From:

Message:

Follow up: Completed: ☐

Phone / Fax / Cell: Email:

Company/Address: Urgency: Low / Medium / High

Date:	Time:	AM / PM	From:

Message:

Follow up: Completed: ☐

Phone / Fax / Cell: Email:

Company/Address: Urgency: Low / Medium / High

Date: Time: AM / PM From:
Message:

Follow up: Completed: ☐
Phone / Fax / Cell: Email:
Company/Address: Urgency: Low / Medium / High

Date: Time: AM / PM From:
Message:

Follow up: Completed: ☐
Phone / Fax / Cell: Email:
Company/Address: Urgency: Low / Medium / High

Date: Time: AM / PM From:
Message:

Follow up: Completed: ☐
Phone / Fax / Cell: Email:
Company/Address: Urgency: Low / Medium / High

Date: Time: AM / PM From:
Message:

Follow up: Completed: ☐
Phone / Fax / Cell: Email:
Company/Address: Urgency: Low / Medium / High

Date: Time: AM / PM From:
Message:

Follow up: Completed: ☐
Phone / Fax / Cell: Email:
Company/Address: Urgency: Low / Medium / High

Date:	Time:	AM / PM	From:

Message:

Follow up:	Completed: ☐

Phone / Fax / Cell:	Email:

Company/Address:	Urgency:	Low / Medium / High

Date:	Time:	AM / PM	From:

Message:

Follow up:	Completed: ☐

Phone / Fax / Cell:	Email:

Company/Address:	Urgency:	Low / Medium / High

Date:	Time:	AM / PM	From:

Message:

Follow up:	Completed: ☐

Phone / Fax / Cell:	Email:

Company/Address:	Urgency:	Low / Medium / High

Date:	Time:	AM / PM	From:

Message:

Follow up:	Completed: ☐

Phone / Fax / Cell:	Email:

Company/Address:	Urgency:	Low / Medium / High

Date:	Time:	AM / PM	From:

Message:

Follow up:	Completed: ☐

Phone / Fax / Cell:	Email:

Company/Address:	Urgency:	Low / Medium / High

Date: Time: AM / PM   From:
Message:

Follow up: Completed: ☐
Phone / Fax / Cell: Email:
Company/Address: Urgency: Low / Medium / High

Date: Time: AM / PM   From:
Message:

Follow up: Completed: ☐
Phone / Fax / Cell: Email:
Company/Address: Urgency: Low / Medium / High

Date: Time: AM / PM   From:
Message:

Follow up: Completed: ☐
Phone / Fax / Cell: Email:
Company/Address: Urgency: Low / Medium / High

Date: Time: AM / PM   From:
Message:

Follow up: Completed: ☐
Phone / Fax / Cell: Email:
Company/Address: Urgency: Low / Medium / High

Date: Time: AM / PM   From:
Message:

Follow up: Completed: ☐
Phone / Fax / Cell: Email:
Company/Address: Urgency: Low / Medium / High

Date: Time: AM / PM   From:
Message:

Follow up: **Completed:** ☐
Phone / Fax / Cell: Email:
Company/Address: Urgency: Low / Medium / High

Date: Time: AM / PM   From:
Message:

Follow up: **Completed:** ☐
Phone / Fax / Cell: Email:
Company/Address: Urgency: Low / Medium / High

Date: Time: AM / PM   From:
Message:

Follow up: **Completed:** ☐
Phone / Fax / Cell: Email:
Company/Address: Urgency: Low / Medium / High

Date: Time: AM / PM   From:
Message:

Follow up: **Completed:** ☐
Phone / Fax / Cell: Email:
Company/Address: Urgency: Low / Medium / High

Date: Time: AM / PM   From:
Message:

Follow up: **Completed:** ☐
Phone / Fax / Cell: Email:
Company/Address: Urgency: Low / Medium / High

Date:　　　　　　　Time:　　　　　　　AM / PM　From:

Message:

Follow up:　　　　　　　　　　　　　　　　　　　　**Completed:** ☐

Phone / Fax / Cell:　　　　　　　　　　Email:

Company/Address:　　　　　　　　　　　　　Urgency:　Low / Medium / High

Date:　　　　　　　Time:　　　　　　　AM / PM　From:

Message:

Follow up:　　　　　　　　　　　　　　　　　　　　**Completed:** ☐

Phone / Fax / Cell:　　　　　　　　　　Email:

Company/Address:　　　　　　　　　　　　　Urgency:　Low / Medium / High

Date:　　　　　　　Time:　　　　　　　AM / PM　From:

Message:

Follow up:　　　　　　　　　　　　　　　　　　　　**Completed:** ☐

Phone / Fax / Cell:　　　　　　　　　　Email:

Company/Address:　　　　　　　　　　　　　Urgency:　Low / Medium / High

Date:　　　　　　　Time:　　　　　　　AM / PM　From:

Message:

Follow up:　　　　　　　　　　　　　　　　　　　　**Completed:** ☐

Phone / Fax / Cell:　　　　　　　　　　Email:

Company/Address:　　　　　　　　　　　　　Urgency:　Low / Medium / High

Date:　　　　　　　Time:　　　　　　　AM / PM　From:

Message:

Follow up:　　　　　　　　　　　　　　　　　　　　**Completed:** ☐

Phone / Fax / Cell:　　　　　　　　　　Email:

Company/Address:　　　　　　　　　　　　　Urgency:　Low / Medium / High

Date: Time: AM / PM   From:
Message:

Follow up: **Completed:**
Phone / Fax / Cell: Email:
Company/Address: Urgency: Low / Medium / High

Date: Time: AM / PM   From:
Message:

Follow up: **Completed:**
Phone / Fax / Cell: Email:
Company/Address: Urgency: Low / Medium / High

Date: Time: AM / PM   From:
Message:

Follow up: **Completed:**
Phone / Fax / Cell: Email:
Company/Address: Urgency: Low / Medium / High

Date: Time: AM / PM   From:
Message:

Follow up: **Completed:**
Phone / Fax / Cell: Email:
Company/Address: Urgency: Low / Medium / High

Date: Time: AM / PM   From:
Message:

Follow up: **Completed:**
Phone / Fax / Cell: Email:
Company/Address: Urgency: Low / Medium / High

Date: Time: AM / PM   From:
Message:

Follow up:			Completed: ☐
Phone / Fax / Cell:		Email:	
Company/Address:		Urgency:	Low / Medium / High

Date: Time: AM / PM   From:
Message:

Follow up:			Completed: ☐
Phone / Fax / Cell:		Email:	
Company/Address:		Urgency:	Low / Medium / High

Date: Time: AM / PM   From:
Message:

Follow up:			Completed: ☐
Phone / Fax / Cell:		Email:	
Company/Address:		Urgency:	Low / Medium / High

Date: Time: AM / PM   From:
Message:

Follow up:			Completed: ☐
Phone / Fax / Cell:		Email:	
Company/Address:		Urgency:	Low / Medium / High

Date: Time: AM / PM   From:
Message:

Follow up:			Completed: ☐
Phone / Fax / Cell:		Email:	
Company/Address:		Urgency:	Low / Medium / High

Date: Time: AM / PM   From:
Message:

Follow up:			Completed:	☐
Phone / Fax / Cell:		Email:		
Company/Address:			Urgency: Low / Medium / High	

Date: Time: AM / PM   From:
Message:

Follow up:			Completed:	☐
Phone / Fax / Cell:		Email:		
Company/Address:			Urgency: Low / Medium / High	

Date: Time: AM / PM   From:
Message:

Follow up:			Completed:	☐
Phone / Fax / Cell:		Email:		
Company/Address:			Urgency: Low / Medium / High	

Date: Time: AM / PM   From:
Message:

Follow up:			Completed:	☐
Phone / Fax / Cell:		Email:		
Company/Address:			Urgency: Low / Medium / High	

Date: Time: AM / PM   From:
Message:

Follow up:			Completed:	☐
Phone / Fax / Cell:		Email:		
Company/Address:			Urgency: Low / Medium / High	

Date:　　　　　　　Time:　　　　　　　AM / PM　From:

Message:

Follow up:　　　　　　　　　　　　　　　　　　　　　　　Completed: ☐

Phone / Fax / Cell:　　　　　　　　　Email:

Company/Address:　　　　　　　　　　　　　　Urgency:　Low / Medium / High

Date:　　　　　　　Time:　　　　　　　AM / PM　From:

Message:

Follow up:　　　　　　　　　　　　　　　　　　　　　　　Completed: ☐

Phone / Fax / Cell:　　　　　　　　　Email:

Company/Address:　　　　　　　　　　　　　　Urgency:　Low / Medium / High

Date:　　　　　　　Time:　　　　　　　AM / PM　From:

Message:

Follow up:　　　　　　　　　　　　　　　　　　　　　　　Completed: ☐

Phone / Fax / Cell:　　　　　　　　　Email:

Company/Address:　　　　　　　　　　　　　　Urgency:　Low / Medium / High

Date:　　　　　　　Time:　　　　　　　AM / PM　From:

Message:

Follow up:　　　　　　　　　　　　　　　　　　　　　　　Completed: ☐

Phone / Fax / Cell:　　　　　　　　　Email:

Company/Address:　　　　　　　　　　　　　　Urgency:　Low / Medium / High

Date:　　　　　　　Time:　　　　　　　AM / PM　From:

Message:

Follow up:　　　　　　　　　　　　　　　　　　　　　　　Completed: ☐

Phone / Fax / Cell:　　　　　　　　　Email:

Company/Address:　　　　　　　　　　　　　　Urgency:　Low / Medium / High

| Date: | Time: | AM / PM | From: |

Message:

| Follow up: | | | Completed: | ☐ |

Phone / Fax / Cell: Email:

Company/Address: Urgency: Low / Medium / High

| Date: | Time: | AM / PM | From: |

Message:

| Follow up: | | | Completed: | ☐ |

Phone / Fax / Cell: Email:

Company/Address: Urgency: Low / Medium / High

| Date: | Time: | AM / PM | From: |

Message:

| Follow up: | | | Completed: | ☐ |

Phone / Fax / Cell: Email:

Company/Address: Urgency: Low / Medium / High

| Date: | Time: | AM / PM | From: |

Message:

| Follow up: | | | Completed: | ☐ |

Phone / Fax / Cell: Email:

Company/Address: Urgency: Low / Medium / High

| Date: | Time: | AM / PM | From: |

Message:

| Follow up: | | | Completed: | ☐ |

Phone / Fax / Cell: Email:

Company/Address: Urgency: Low / Medium / High

Date: Time: AM / PM   From:
Message:

Follow up: Completed: ☐
Phone / Fax / Cell: Email:
Company/Address: Urgency: Low / Medium / High

Date: Time: AM / PM   From:
Message:

Follow up: Completed: ☐
Phone / Fax / Cell: Email:
Company/Address: Urgency: Low / Medium / High

Date: Time: AM / PM   From:
Message:

Follow up: Completed: ☐
Phone / Fax / Cell: Email:
Company/Address: Urgency: Low / Medium / High

Date: Time: AM / PM   From:
Message:

Follow up: Completed: ☐
Phone / Fax / Cell: Email:
Company/Address: Urgency: Low / Medium / High

Date: Time: AM / PM   From:
Message:

Follow up: Completed: ☐
Phone / Fax / Cell: Email:
Company/Address: Urgency: Low / Medium / High

Date:	Time:	AM / PM	From:
Message:

Follow up:			Completed:	☐
Phone / Fax / Cell:			Email:
Company/Address:			Urgency:	Low / Medium / High

Date:	Time:	AM / PM	From:
Message:

Follow up:			Completed:	☐
Phone / Fax / Cell:			Email:
Company/Address:			Urgency:	Low / Medium / High

Date:	Time:	AM / PM	From:
Message:

Follow up:			Completed:	☐
Phone / Fax / Cell:			Email:
Company/Address:			Urgency:	Low / Medium / High

Date:	Time:	AM / PM	From:
Message:

Follow up:			Completed:	☐
Phone / Fax / Cell:			Email:
Company/Address:			Urgency:	Low / Medium / High

Date:	Time:	AM / PM	From:
Message:

Follow up:			Completed:	☐
Phone / Fax / Cell:			Email:
Company/Address:			Urgency:	Low / Medium / High

Date: Time: AM / PM   From:
Message:

Follow up:				Completed:	☐

Phone / Fax / Cell: Email:
Company/Address: Urgency: Low / Medium / High

Date: Time: AM / PM   From:
Message:

Follow up:				Completed:	☐

Phone / Fax / Cell: Email:
Company/Address: Urgency: Low / Medium / High

Date: Time: AM / PM   From:
Message:

Follow up:				Completed:	☐

Phone / Fax / Cell: Email:
Company/Address: Urgency: Low / Medium / High

Date: Time: AM / PM   From:
Message:

Follow up:				Completed:	☐

Phone / Fax / Cell: Email:
Company/Address: Urgency: Low / Medium / High

Date: Time: AM / PM   From:
Message:

Follow up:				Completed:	☐

Phone / Fax / Cell: Email:
Company/Address: Urgency: Low / Medium / High

Date: Time: AM / PM From:
Message:

Follow up:		Completed:	
Phone / Fax / Cell:		Email:	
Company/Address:		Urgency: Low / Medium / High	

Date: Time: AM / PM From:
Message:

Follow up:		Completed:	
Phone / Fax / Cell:		Email:	
Company/Address:		Urgency: Low / Medium / High	

Date: Time: AM / PM From:
Message:

Follow up:		Completed:	
Phone / Fax / Cell:		Email:	
Company/Address:		Urgency: Low / Medium / High	

Date: Time: AM / PM From:
Message:

Follow up:		Completed:	
Phone / Fax / Cell:		Email:	
Company/Address:		Urgency: Low / Medium / High	

Date: Time: AM / PM From:
Message:

Follow up:		Completed:	
Phone / Fax / Cell:		Email:	
Company/Address:		Urgency: Low / Medium / High	

Date: Time: AM / PM   From:
Message:

Follow up:			Completed: ☐
Phone / Fax / Cell:		Email:	
Company/Address:		Urgency:	Low / Medium / High

Date: Time: AM / PM   From:
Message:

Follow up:			Completed: ☐
Phone / Fax / Cell:		Email:	
Company/Address:		Urgency:	Low / Medium / High

Date: Time: AM / PM   From:
Message:

Follow up:			Completed: ☐
Phone / Fax / Cell:		Email:	
Company/Address:		Urgency:	Low / Medium / High

Date: Time: AM / PM   From:
Message:

Follow up:			Completed: ☐
Phone / Fax / Cell:		Email:	
Company/Address:		Urgency:	Low / Medium / High

Date: Time: AM / PM   From:
Message:

Follow up:			Completed: ☐
Phone / Fax / Cell:		Email:	
Company/Address:		Urgency:	Low / Medium / High

| Date: | Time: | AM / PM | From: |

Message:

Follow up: **Completed:** ☐

Phone / Fax / Cell: Email:

Company/Address: Urgency: Low / Medium / High

| Date: | Time: | AM / PM | From: |

Message:

Follow up: **Completed:** ☐

Phone / Fax / Cell: Email:

Company/Address: Urgency: Low / Medium / High

| Date: | Time: | AM / PM | From: |

Message:

Follow up: **Completed:** ☐

Phone / Fax / Cell: Email:

Company/Address: Urgency: Low / Medium / High

| Date: | Time: | AM / PM | From: |

Message:

Follow up: **Completed:** ☐

Phone / Fax / Cell: Email:

Company/Address: Urgency: Low / Medium / High

| Date: | Time: | AM / PM | From: |

Message:

Follow up: **Completed:** ☐

Phone / Fax / Cell: Email:

Company/Address: Urgency: Low / Medium / High

Date:　　　　　　　　Time:　　　　　　　　AM / PM　From:

Message:

Follow up:　　　　　　　　　　　　　　　　　　　　**Completed:** ☐

Phone / Fax / Cell:　　　　　　　　　　　Email:

Company/Address:　　　　　　　　　　　　　　Urgency:　Low / Medium / High

Date:　　　　　　　　Time:　　　　　　　　AM / PM　From:

Message:

Follow up:　　　　　　　　　　　　　　　　　　　　**Completed:** ☐

Phone / Fax / Cell:　　　　　　　　　　　Email:

Company/Address:　　　　　　　　　　　　　　Urgency:　Low / Medium / High

Date:　　　　　　　　Time:　　　　　　　　AM / PM　From:

Message:

Follow up:　　　　　　　　　　　　　　　　　　　　**Completed:** ☐

Phone / Fax / Cell:　　　　　　　　　　　Email:

Company/Address:　　　　　　　　　　　　　　Urgency:　Low / Medium / High

Date:　　　　　　　　Time:　　　　　　　　AM / PM　From:

Message:

Follow up:　　　　　　　　　　　　　　　　　　　　**Completed:** ☐

Phone / Fax / Cell:　　　　　　　　　　　Email:

Company/Address:　　　　　　　　　　　　　　Urgency:　Low / Medium / High

Date:　　　　　　　　Time:　　　　　　　　AM / PM　From:

Message:

Follow up:　　　　　　　　　　　　　　　　　　　　**Completed:** ☐

Phone / Fax / Cell:　　　　　　　　　　　Email:

Company/Address:　　　　　　　　　　　　　　Urgency:　Low / Medium / High

| Date: | Time: | AM / PM | From: |

Message:

Follow up: Completed: ☐

Phone / Fax / Cell: Email:

Company/Address: Urgency: Low / Medium / High

| Date: | Time: | AM / PM | From: |

Message:

Follow up: Completed: ☐

Phone / Fax / Cell: Email:

Company/Address: Urgency: Low / Medium / High

| Date: | Time: | AM / PM | From: |

Message:

Follow up: Completed: ☐

Phone / Fax / Cell: Email:

Company/Address: Urgency: Low / Medium / High

| Date: | Time: | AM / PM | From: |

Message:

Follow up: Completed: ☐

Phone / Fax / Cell: Email:

Company/Address: Urgency: Low / Medium / High

| Date: | Time: | AM / PM | From: |

Message:

Follow up: Completed: ☐

Phone / Fax / Cell: Email:

Company/Address: Urgency: Low / Medium / High

Date:　　　　　　　Time:　　　　　　　AM / PM　From:

Message:

Follow up:			Completed: ☐
Phone / Fax / Cell:		Email:	
Company/Address:		Urgency:	Low / Medium / High

Date:　　　　　　　Time:　　　　　　　AM / PM　From:

Message:

Follow up:			Completed: ☐
Phone / Fax / Cell:		Email:	
Company/Address:		Urgency:	Low / Medium / High

Date:　　　　　　　Time:　　　　　　　AM / PM　From:

Message:

Follow up:			Completed: ☐
Phone / Fax / Cell:		Email:	
Company/Address:		Urgency:	Low / Medium / High

Date:　　　　　　　Time:　　　　　　　AM / PM　From:

Message:

Follow up:			Completed: ☐
Phone / Fax / Cell:		Email:	
Company/Address:		Urgency:	Low / Medium / High

Date:	Time:	AM / PM	From:

Message:

Follow up: Completed: ☐

Phone / Fax / Cell: Email:

Company/Address: Urgency: Low / Medium / High

Date:	Time:	AM / PM	From:

Message:

Follow up: Completed: ☐

Phone / Fax / Cell: Email:

Company/Address: Urgency: Low / Medium / High

Date:	Time:	AM / PM	From:

Message:

Follow up: Completed: ☐

Phone / Fax / Cell: Email:

Company/Address: Urgency: Low / Medium / High

Date:	Time:	AM / PM	From:

Message:

Follow up: Completed: ☐

Phone / Fax / Cell: Email:

Company/Address: Urgency: Low / Medium / High

Date:	Time:	AM / PM	From:

Message:

Follow up: Completed: ☐

Phone / Fax / Cell: Email:

Company/Address: Urgency: Low / Medium / High

All rights reserved. No part of this publication may be reproduced, distributed, or transmitted in any form or by any means, including photocopying, recording, or other electronic or mechanical methods, without the prior written permission of the publisher, except in the case of brief quotations embodied in critical reviews and certain other noncommercial uses permitted by copyright law.

Designed and created using resources from: pixabay.com, freepik.com/pikisuperstar, unsplash.com

Made in the USA
Coppell, TX
31 August 2022